DISCOVER THE MIRACLE IN YOUR HOUSE

10 PRINCIPLES OF
A BREAKTHROUGH LIFE

JOSEPH WILSON
DIEDRE A. WILSON

dustjacket

Published by Dust Jacket Press
*Discover the Miracle in Your House: 10 Principles of a Breakthrough Life /
Joseph Wilson and Diedre A. Wilson*

Dust Jacket Press
P. O. Box 721243
Oklahoma City, OK 73172
www.dustjacket.com

All Scripture quotations not otherwise designated are from the King James Version of the Bible.

Permission to quote from the following copyrighted versions of the Bible is acknowledged with appreciation:

The Message (MSG). Copyright ©1993, 1994, 1995, 1996, 2000, 2001, 2002 by Eugene H. Peterson.

The Holy Bible, New International Version®, NIV® Copyright ©1973, 1978, 1984, 2011 by Biblica, Inc.® Used by permission. All rights reserved worldwide.

New King James Version® (NKJV). Copyright ©1982 by Thomas Nelson. Used by permission. All rights reserved.

Dust Jacket logos are registered trademarks of Dust Jacket Press, Inc.

Cover & interior design: D. E. West / ZAQ Designs & Dust Jacket Creative Services

Printed in the United States of America

www.dustjacket.com

DEDICATION

Edith Wilson Statham—in memory and honor of my sister "Edie," who was both tough and tender, which helped her to be a great mother and grandmother, excel as a leader in the workplace, and pursue God with a determined drive.

Willie James Pendleton Jr.—in memory and honor of my brother "Willie," who was intelligent, steady, and compassionate. He was an attentive husband and dad who demonstrated resiliency in life and the determination to finish strong.

CONTENTS

It is rare for me to say that I know people who are heroes of our Christian faith—heroes of leadership, family, marriage, business, church development, and kingdom economics. In Diedre and Joe Wilson I can authentically say I know true heroes.

I have known Joe and Diedre—"Dee," as I used to call her in our days at Baldwin-Wallace University—for over thirty-seven years. In that time I have seen them both grow from embryonic college freshmen, with an edge to them, to transformational servant leaders and change agents.

This transformation from edgy college freshmen to global icons of excellence did not happen overnight. It has a been a steady yet dynamic *process* of learning, unlearning, and relearning lessons from God and life itself.

The process of greatness means being gripped, stripped, ripped, flipped, whipped, dipped, equipped, and then finally shipped to one's ultimate destiny. Joe and Diedre have lived it and have the credibility and virtue to write about it.

Joe and Diedre's lives reflect the process God takes people through who are willing to grow and risk it all for His glory and to be used in mighty ways to change the world.

In their new book, *Discover the Miracle in Your House: 10 Principles of a Breakthrough Life,* Joe and Diedre lay out a lucid roadmap for how to avoid the breakdown cycle of despair and failure and how to achieve systematic breakthrough in business, ministry, marriage, and finance.

What is so beautiful about this writing is what it is not. It is not some esoteric, obtuse, pedantic, academic, theoretical prose full of intellectually unproven jargon. Rather, it is a real exposé of two people who met under challenging circumstances in the inner city of Cleveland and surrendered their lives to God and then discovered, dreamed, designed, and delivered on a masterpiece of practical, applicable, experiential genius that will refurbish and renovate one's head, heart, hands, and habits if it is read and applied.

This book is divinely inspired to empower generations of leaders to embrace what God has put right before them to embrace the set time, survive the meantime, and to be readied for the appointed time of destiny.

I promise that you will love this book and will read it over and over again to gain fresh revelation and inspiration from this message of incremental improvement being better than postponed perfection.

With gratitude and love I endorse Joe and Diedre's magnificent work.

Dr. Ronaldo Archer
Chairman and CEO
The Places of HOPE
www.theplacesofhope.com

ACKNOWLEDGMENTS

Joseph Bucholtz—We are tremendously grateful for my dad's love, encouragement, affirmation, and the wisdom he shared when we were challenged with getting started and unsure of how we were going to achieve this book.

John C. Maxwell—I am grateful for the mentorship I receive from John that challenges me to constantly grow and exceed expectations and the perspective I gain as he shares his rich experience that offers me hope and a sense of normalcy as I develop as a leader.

Stan Toler—my late friend who encouraged me from the very beginning and always expressed a genuine excitement to be in my company. The times Stan and I presented together were invaluable to my development in training churches. God used him mightily to help me embrace the next season of ministry leadership.

Adam Toler, COO Dustjacket—a great publishing resource that helped this work become possible; we feel extremely blessed working with him as he bears the generous spirit of his late father, Stan.

Jonathan Wright—provided the editing and formatting for this project with a caring nature not just for the book but also in demonstrating his concern for us by setting our expectations and working diligently amidst challenging circumstances.

Paul Martinelli, president of the John Maxwell Team—a great thinking partner who has helped me grow in my ability as a business strategist with courage and determination that rise above my self-limiting beliefs to achieve new levels of success.

Marsha Myhand—a gifted writer who has helped us achieve success with several books and has outdone herself with this one. Thank you for your willingness to partner with us to advance God's kingdom and change the lives of people around the globe.

Nadia Nichols—a consummate professional with a strong sense of commitment who has helped us edit and gain perspective on several works.

Alan and Vivienne Costner—We are grateful for your friendship and walking this journey with us as ministry and business advisors and strategists.

Liz Myers—Your willingness to contribute your ability in the area of strategic implementation helps us go from dream to reality.

Dane and Lisa Clark—true friends and thinking partners who help us navigate the twists and turns of kingdom ministry and know how to discern the season and what to do according to the heart of God.

DeAngelo Malcolm—a successful entrepreneur and emerging ministry leader who challenges me to keep growing to keep pace as his mentor and help him rise to the level of his greatness.

Carl and DeShawn Jackson—our great friends and growth partners who allow us to be authentic and encourage us not to get stuck at levels we should be growing through.

Kenny Williams—has challenged us to be clear about our purpose and be committed to it even when others are not prepared to share the same passion and drive.

Derrick Taylor—an invaluable voice from God who uses his spiritual gifts to speak the heart of God providing confirmation and guidance in challenging times.

PREFACE

You're invited to look inside a window into a world from the advantage of someone else's situation and learn how to navigate your life of tragedies, triumphs, and treasure development by learning how to apply any and all of these ten principles. We each possess unique stories and situations and therefore may not relate directly to the story of this widow, who was left without basic support.

But you can readily relate to when the bottom falls out and you need immediate help to develop solutions that will get you back on your feet and enable you to overcome and experience the joy of a breakthrough life. It's not uncommon in times of crisis to feel as if one break, one turn of events or opportunity will position you to start living the life you've dreamed about again.

THE STORY

One day the wife of a man from the guild of prophets called out to Elisha, "Your servant my husband is dead. You well know what a good man he was, devoted to God. And now the man to whom he was in debt is on his way to collect by taking my two children as slaves."

Elisha said, "I wonder how I can be of help. Tell me, what do you have in your house?"

"Nothing," she said. "Well, I do have a little oil."

"Here's what you do," said Elisha. "Go up and down the street and borrow jugs and bowls from all your neighbors. And not just a few—all you can get. Then come home and lock the door behind you, you and your sons. Pour oil into each container; when each is full, set it aside."

She did what he said. She locked the door behind her and her sons; as they brought the containers to her, she filled them. When all the jugs and bowls were full, she said to one of her sons, "Another jug, please."

He said, "That's it. There are no more jugs."

Then the oil stopped.

She went and told the story to the man of God. He said, "Go sell the oil and make good on your debts. Live, both you and your sons, on what's left."
(2 Kings 4:1–7 MSG)

This story of the widow is an example of one's struggle with the concept of faith. What is faith? Why do I need to have it? How can I apply it to my life?

Although Scripture says that her husband was a "good man, devoted to God," it doesn't explicitly indicate that she was a believer or a "good woman devoted to God." However, given that she sought the prophet, Elisha, lets us know that she had some idea of where to get help.

Newly widowed, left with two sons to raise, and facing mounting debt that she was now obligated to pay, the woman had few options. Not knowing if anyone would be willing to help her, she began a walk of faith with that initial step. She sought the prophet's help to figure out what to do and how the God he served and to whom her husband was devoted might provide the miracle she needed to survive.

While the Bible is silent as to the length of her journey of faith, we do know that her obedience to the prophet's instructions led to a soul-searching period of discovery. What has emerged from her response to "Tell me, what do you have in your house?" are the *ten principles of a breakthrough life.* These ten necessary habits if embraced and applied to your life can help you celebrate your value, advance your cause, and fulfill your purpose.

INTRODUCTION

How could a little oil in a jar not only prevent a grieving family from being evicted—or in this story, from becoming indentured servants—but also sustain them over time? A widow and her two sons sought the counsel of a well-regarded prophet, who gave them a simple life-changing plan, which at first seemed absurd.

"Go up and down the street and borrow jugs and bowls from all your neighbors. And not just a few—all you can get. Then come home and lock the door behind you, you and your sons. Pour oil into each container; when each is full, set it aside."

Can you imagine going door to door in your neighborhood asking to borrow empty jars, jugs, or bowls—gathering containers that were likely of different dimensions, colors, shapes, and weights?

But she did. Once they were gathered, she poured oil into each one. She did this until there were no more jugs. Then the oil stopped. Scripture does not say how many containers were filled. She returned to the prophet to explain what she had done. His reply:

> *"Go and sell the oil and make good on your debts. Live, both you and your sons, on what's left."*

It was nothing short of a miracle.

How did she do it? Was it really that simple? Was her faith in the prophet, in herself, her sons, or God? The story doesn't include this information.

What we do know, however, is that because of her obedience and follow-through with the prophet, she was able to pay off her husband's debts and continue to provide for herself and her sons "on what's left." The prophet helped her change how she felt about her situation to focus on the facts of her situation by asking the question "What do you have in your house?" This question initiated her journey to living in the overflow—the process of going from apparent disaster to affluence or overflowing abundance.

Discover the Miracle in Your House explores the unanswered question *How did she do it?* Scripture tells us what she did but doesn't provide the details of how this miracle was accomplished. Using the biblical narrative as the backdrop, *Discover the Miracle in Your House* will help you discover and apply the necessary life habits that will enable you to have a breakthrough life. You'll be able to identify the skills and talents you have so that you can overcome the obstacles that prevent you from fulfilling your potential, reaching your goals, and achieving your long-held dreams.

Discover the Miracle in Your House will show you how to assess, value, and apply your skills and the knowledge God has outlined for you. Let's begin by asking as the prophet did: *What's in your house?*

1

Assess Your Situation: Take Inventory

The manufacturing plant where you've worked for fifteen years has relocated to another state and you have decided not to uproot your family and disrupt your children's schooling. You opt instead to take a severance package and believe you'll find another comparable job nearby. Several months have passed. You are still out of work and your finances have begun to take a hit.

A company-wide reorganization has left you without a title and a position. The company has vowed to retain you and other employees, provided your skills set fit in with the new direction it planned to take. But apparently that's not happening.

You are nearing three months behind in your rent. You have cobbled together money from friends and family but your landlord is growing impatient and his forbearance from evicting you is starting to wane.

You are a single mom with two young sons. Your husband has just died and you learn that he had tremendous debts; you have few resources from which to pay them. Distraught and unsure of where to turn, you seek guidance from your husband's boss, a man who knew your husband intimately and greatly respected him. You offer desperate pleas for help, reminding the man of your husband's dedication, diligence, and integrity.

These anecdotes may sound familiar because they reflect the circumstances many of us find ourselves in, sometimes through unfortunate circumstances and others from poor decision-making.

Through these *10 Principles of a Breakthrough Life* you will learn how to uncover and discover life habits that perpetuate the breakthrough life that you will use repeatedly throughout your life.

Each principle is a type of self-discovery or rediscovery— of who you are, what you have, how to understand and appraise what you have, how to value yourself, and how others might benefit from what you offer.

For this to happen in our own lives, we must be good stewards over what we have accumulated. We also must recognize that "value" is not only currency. If we place value only on currency, then we miss the value of things that can lead to material and spiritual wealth.

TAKE INVENTORY

When the prophet asked the woman, "What do you have in your house?" she paused for a moment. Her first reply was "Nothing." Then after another brief pause she said, "Well, I do have a little oil."

The widow needed to pay off her husband's debts or face dire consequences. She had no money with which to do it and therefore concluded she didn't have anything of value.

We need to be careful of the value we place on money, on currency. There is a danger in thinking money/currency is the only thing to value and if we don't have it or have cash on hand, then somehow we have nothing of value. If we place value only on currency, then we miss the value of things that can lead to the currency/cash that we need.

The question the prophet posed, "What do you have in your house?" is an opportunity for you to take inventory not just of your material possessions but also of the skills you have.

The concept of "house" represents both the *physical* and the *spiritual.* A house is a building for human habitation, especially one that is lived in by a family or a small group of people. It's a dwelling place. A person might live in a bungalow on a quiet cul-de-sac or in a cozy farmhouse in a rural community. In Scripture we are referred to as a dwelling place or the temple of the living God. We can be the living quarters for God:

What? know ye not that your body is the temple of the Holy Ghost which is in you, which ye have of God, and ye are not your own? For ye are bought with a price: therefore glorify God in your body, and in your spirit, which are God's.

(1 Corinthians 6:19–20)

A house also can represent a gathering place, such as a church, as it is often called "the house of God." This is typically where unrelated people spend time together in worship and fellowship.

As you take inventory, check your physical *and* your spiritual house because God has things in both. You need to spend time in and with both.

Why? Sometimes we have "stuff" in our house that we can't see. They are hidden on purpose, through neglect, or even because of forgetfulness. But if we spend enough time in the house—the home or the church, for example, alone or with others—we might find that things we've been praying about and asking God for may already be in the house.

The solution may be sitting across from you at the table or in the pew. The solution may be sitting next to you on the bus or standing in front of you in line at the grocery store. If you check the house, you might make an amazing discovery of what God has for you, the very thing you overlooked or disregarded.

Remember that what God has for you—He has for *you*. Don't think that anyone else can come into your house and lay claim to what is divinely yours. God is not going to bless someone else with what He has assigned as yours.

The widow went to the prophet in what she believed was a crisis situation. With her husband now dead, she felt she was at the brink of losing everything.

But this wasn't the real crisis.

Too often we focus on the "surface" things in our lives rather than the real issues. We can clean up the surfaces, vacuum away the dirt, mop the floors—and still not realize that we have termites that will inevitably bring the whole house down.

No matter how clean the outside is or how pretty it looks, we must get to the root of the problem. For the widow the real crisis was that she did not know how to get to her true value by herself.

DISCOVERING WHO
OR WHAT IS NECESSARY

The widow, however, went the right place to find out—she went to God. And God has "necessary others" all around us who will help us navigate to get to where God wants us to be, to help us do and experience so much through Him. For the widow, the prophet served as the "necessary other" to help her get past the loss of her husband and try to rebuild her life. Sometimes we can go only so far by ourselves.

What do you do when you get to the end of yourself, when you have done and given all you believe you can?

Do you stop? Do you remain stuck in that place of bewilderment? Or do you try to seek outside help so that you can go further? Consider how the church, a job, the community can become that "necessary other" for you.

You may be involved in a civic organization or are a member of a church or community group. All of these and other similar connections have value. And they offer opportunities for you to learn things about yourself, to be inspired by what they do and how they do it. The fact you are connected shows *your* value.

LOOK FOR THE EXTRAORDINARY

We too need to find ways to navigate through the difficult challenges of the 21st century in order to get where God wants us to be.

As we take inventory of what we have, we should be looking for the miracles, the supernatural things in the house. A miracle is something that is supernatural—it's not ordinary.

For example, it's a miracle to buy a car when you have no money in the bank. It's not a miracle to buy a car when you have a job and money in the bank to pay for it. That's a blessing. The blessing is that you have the job and the income available to buy a new car. But when you are diagnosed with a rare disease and there is no cure for it—and you get healed—that's a miracle.

The widow woman, like many people, needed a miracle. She first had to take careful inventory of her house. She was unable to see that she was in line for a supernatural miracle because she overlooked the very thing in her house that could make a difference.

So, you too must go through this period of inventory. Part of this process is evaluating your situation and asking questions. Ask yourself, *What do I have? What's in my house? What's in my hand? What's in my heart? What are my habits? What do I own that I can use to create my best future? What are my assets? What's missing?*

Let's define *asset* in a functional way. It is simply a useful and desirable item or quality. It doesn't always have to deal with money, stocks, or bonds.

You will need to look for those things that you can get rid of so you can discover what is valuable. Once you know what you have, you can move forward.

With the prophet's help, the woman took inventory. They worked together to evaluate her situation. They began to look at her assets, her useful and desirable qualities.

Although the widow was devastated and destitute, the prophet helped her explore her possibilities. He also connected her to God, who was more than enough. Her possibilities exploded because she was now in a place where she could clearly think through her predicament, evaluate her circumstances, and take a closer look at the useful and desirable things of quality—the assets—she had.

As you check your house, you have to be there long enough to discover those things, the "stuff" that may be of value as well as those things that may have hindered you and kept you from moving forward.

UNCOVERING YOUR ASSETS

Checking your inventory requires you to have some "me time." From a spiritual standpoint ask yourself, *What are the things in my house—within me— that are getting in the way of progress? What do I already have that can take me to the next level? What am I missing that is preventing me from moving forward?*

You may have to shut the door to your house; seek quiet moments for prayer and meditation. Use this period of inventory for self-reflection and self-evaluation.

Recognize that we are all created in the image of God. Yet each of us is unique, so much so that, as Jesus said in Luke 12:7, *"The very hairs of your head are all numbered. Do not fear therefore; you are of more value than many sparrows"* (NKJV). Look at your talents, your abilities, your interests, your habits. These comprise who you are.

As you take inventory, as you ask yourself these and other questions, as you assess the situations in your life and the circumstances and talents and abilities, what you are working toward is finding your best fit.

For help go to https://uniquelyyou.org/coach/Power-2Become.

Initially you know a little something about a given situation or need and you can get a few things accomplished, so it fits. But it's short term. You aren't able to do it forever; you do it because it's needed and it's necessary for you to grow.

You move from that to a good fit, meaning that you are moving closer to what really feels like who you are. It can be difficult at times figuring out what you like and don't like, what you can handle and what would be causing your stress.

What you want, however, is your best fit. You want it to feel natural, authentic, that you are doing things in a way that feels comfortable to you. You are doing things properly. You are operating at your full potential.

But to get there you must take inventory. You must check the house. You must uncover the hidden assets and then begin assessing their true value.

2

Appraise Your True Value:
Value What You Have

Once you have assessed your situation or checked the house, you can begin to appraise your true value. The words of 2 Kings 4:2 provide a way to talk about appraising your true value, because sometimes you're the last to see your worth. Others can see it and recognize it before you do.

But you must be careful. Sometimes people can position your true value to benefit others. Other times they approach it selfishly and seek to take advantage of you *for their good.* You might never find out this is happening and they won't tell you because it would ruin their good thing.

The prophet in his conversation with the widow woman seeks to help her assess her true value. He asks, "*What shall I do for thee? tell me, what hast thou in the house?*" Her reply: "*Thine handmaid hath not any thing in the house, save a pot of oil.*"

We understand her predicament and those of others who are dealing with a great loss. We also know that she has a lot of resources in her house—she just can't see it. She is not able to comprehend all she has. However, she pauses before she replies when she says, "save" ("but"), suggesting that there just may be something in the house after all.

We must get to the place where we allow God to eliminate things in our lives—the stuff—that prevents us from moving forward, from taking risks, from changing course.

Consider times when you have prayed and/or fasted, believing and trusting God for something only to discover that He was not moving because you already had what you needed. What you needed was already at your disposal, already within you.

While you may not appreciate that kind of struggle, understand that the beauty is in the search; the power is in the finding. This process is much better, much deeper than God just giving it to you.

We sometimes overlook what we perceive to be the small things God places in our lives. When you discover them, they might not appear to be much by themselves, but when placed in God's hands, under His power they are already more than enough.

You must be careful not to place your faith in the "too little" rather than in the God who is more than enough. It is easy to get locked into thinking of what you don't have, what it can't produce, or what you can't achieve. As a result, you'll overlook what you do have.

The widow woman's situation is common to all of us. As the prophet calls her to search, discover, and make decisions, so too God is calling us to do the same thing: to appraise the true value of what we have.

THINK LIKE AN APPRAISER

The woman had oil. What was it worth? What was its true value? She now had to develop an opinion of the value of what she possessed.

How often do we accept other people's opinions and disregard our own? How often do we rely on what others say rather than developing our own opinion? Sure—there is a time to seek other people's opinions, yet if you rely solely on what others say, you will never truly understand the value of your own opinion or be able to develop the confidence and authority to move it forward.

When you defer to what others say, you may have such thoughts as *Is it really true? Am I going to come out okay? Will this work?* But when you develop your own opinion, even if the situation does not end as you envisioned, you are still vested in it because it's your opinion. You own it.

How do you get to that level of confidence? Learn how to appraise. Learn how to think like an appraiser. To develop an opinion of value or of what something is worth, you must

1. Provide an objective, impartial, and unbiased opinion. This requires investigation and reflection about what you own.

2. Provide assistance to those who own, manage, sell, invest, or lend. You start to gather more information to determine the value of what you have.

3. Assemble a series of facts, statistics, and other details regarding specific things about what you own. This will generate fact-based information to help you better examine others' opinions. You'll begin to look at what others have said and the conclusions they have made. You may start to see trends and the factors that led an item to increase—or decrease— in value over time.

4. Analyze the data. Genuinely take a deep dive into the information you've assembled. Look at who is saying what and what they are saying. Look at the information with a critical eye, because in the end you must have the confidence to move forward.

5. Develop an opinion of the value. Draw a conclusion that you can live with, regardless of what others say. If you have done the proper appraisal, you'll be able to assign a true value.

Why is this process important? You must become confident in who you are and what you have in your house in order to recognize the value and worth of it.

To become a true appraiser of your own true value, you must grow. You must learn and acquire more information about yourself in order to have your value increase. You can't rely on the opinions of others, the opinions of last year, or your achievements of five or ten years ago. You must look at where you are now.

Consider matters dealing with home ownership. Each time an addition or update is made to the house, its value increases. Unless you report the improvements to the county auditor's office, they will not know that the value of your home should be increased. They are often using data based only on market trends.

It's important to examine and appraise your true value from time to time. People update their résumés to elaborate on their work experiences, skills, achievements, awards, research, or service. If you neglect to make this type of self-examination, you won't show up in full value and others will be free to devalue you.

As you undergo this self-appraisal, it is important that you also exercise sound judgment. In other words, as the apostle Paul shares in Romans 12:3, *I say . . . to every man that is among you, not to think of himself more highly than he ought to think; but to think soberly, according as God hath dealt to every man the measure of faith.*

While it is important that you develop confidence in your opinion and your true value, it also is important that you let others praise you. If their praise is true and sincere, people will see your value. It will mean that your value is on display and others will benefit from it and celebrate it.

As your confidence grows, as you learn and continue to acquire information about yourself, you can then begin to communicate this process with others. You'll be able to share the benefits of becoming an appraiser because you have experienced it for yourself.

MAINTAIN THE PROPER PERSPECTIVE

Remember that it is God who is doing a great thing in you; it is because God is great, not you.

As you acknowledge God, you can move about freely knowing your worth and not allowing anyone to devalue you. Unlike the arrogance on display by many people in power, the confidence you now have is based on what God has given you and has done on your behalf.

This recognition of your true value can inspire others. Many people need value deposited into them, and what you now have can and should be shared with others. It's knowing that if it had not been for God, you would be stuck where you are.

Much like the widow woman, had the prophet not told her to "check the house," she may have remained in her grief-stricken, debt-ridden state. Instead, she mustered the courage to check her house, analyze what she possessed, and agree to abide by the prophet's instructions. So should we.

KNOW YOUR TRUE VALUE.
DISCOVER YOUR PURPOSE.

God, the Creator of all living things, has given each of us what I term a "God DNA." It represents the nucleus, the foundation of who we are. God has determined that He wants a certain thing from each of us. We carry His DNA on the earth and it develops our passion. It is why there are some things you can leave alone, while other things you can't as they keep calling you, pulling you, compelling you, and drawing you toward a certain result. He doesn't force you. He creates a passion for it within you because it matches where He's taking you. This passion turns into discovering your true purpose.

It is essential once you learn your true value that you own it. As you develop your purpose, others will begin to discover why you are here. Others around you will recognize that you are assigned to supply something in their lives. They will discover your purpose and celebrate your presence.

Ultimately you will need to understand your purpose and that it grows out of your "God DNA." Again, this requires a careful appraisal. Continue to check your house and look at what might appear ordinary, too little, or insufficient and allow God to do something miraculous with it. Go to https://uniquelyyou.org/coach/Power2Become and discover your "God DNA."

Lock into your "God DNA." Even when it appears that you are stalled or parked for a while, your "God DNA" is still in motion. When God has parked you, it means things are happening that He doesn't want you to be a part of or in the middle of.

In those parked moments, reflect. Consider why God has parked you. Is there something in your life you need to get rid of? Is there something that is interfering with your progress? Use this opportunity to determine what it is that you need to leave behind so that you can be ready to move and align yourself at the right time. When the time is right, you'll re-engage because it is time for you to move forward. Let your life grow out of your "God DNA" and your life will grow into the plan God has for you.

3

Affirm Your Present:
Effectively Use What You Have to Advance
Your Cause/Purpose

You'll often find that the more you check your house the more things you will discover and uncover about yourself and about the things you own, whether natural, tangible, or spiritual. Sometimes what you uncover might appear simple, small, or insignificant. That's largely because you have failed to pause long enough to assess its true value.

You can easily miss God and what He might be saying because you are not focused on the present.

The widow woman at first glance thought that all she had was a little oil. But the prophet encouraged her to look again, to check the house because there was more than what she perceived.

Indeed, in the latter part of 2 Kings 4:1 it is inferred that the woman had something of value. Although she didn't know the totality of what she possessed, the creditors did. It's implied in her statement *"The creditor has come to take unto him my two sons to be bondmen."*

The creditors were coming to take her two sons and put them into indentured servitude. Her sons represented tremendous value but the widow woman couldn't see it. She discounted their worth and focused on her inability to pay—financially—for her husband's debt. But her sons were extremely valuable, which is why the creditors wanted them.

Scripture does not state what gifts or talents her sons had or what type of work they were capable of doing. Yet the creditors knew they would benefit greatly and achieve more if they had her sons in servitude. And as the story unfolds, we begin to see just how valuable they were.

But their mother was so overwhelmed with loss that she missed it.

The oil represented the commodity; her sons represented the physical resource that would allow them to reap financial benefits.

EXAMINE YOUR RESOURCES

Before you move forward with any plan, it is important that you examine all your available resources. In other words, *check your house.* Look at the people who are with you. Look at the people you are connected with—whether in your home, the church, your neighborhood, or even via social media. Instead of minimizing or dismissing people based on who you think they are or what you think they can do, go back and look at their true value. You might miss a great experience or disregard an opportunity with someone because of a disagreement or putting too much emphasis on his or her shortcomings.

Don't get so caught up in the disagreement or the shortcoming that you miss the value within it. Until you recognize silver as valuable, you'll never get the tarnish off of it because it will never seem to be worth the effort. You won't want to go through the process of removing the tarnish because of the amount of time it will take. Yet once you realize its value, you won't mind expending the time or the cost to get it right.

Be sure you don't miss what is right in front of you. Don't miss the gifts. Don't miss the talents. Don't miss the capacity. Don't miss the potential. Don't overlook other people around you or those you are connected with—because there are some things you can learn from them that you have been longing for.

USE WHAT'S AVAILABLE

The widow woman had not quite come to terms with her situation. She hadn't yet recognized the value of the oil or the value of her sons. Both were overlooked and discounted. The oil was available. Her sons were available. The challenge for her was discovering how they could make a difference in their situation.

Have you ever really, really needed the help of someone who you knew could do the kind of job you needed to have done? You might hear, "As much as I want to, I can't right now."

You are inconvenienced and may suffer because the person isn't available. You have to wait. Whatever the time frame, availability becomes a significant resource. Time is a powerful tool and a resource to God. You must look at your availability critically and make some difficult decisions as to what you will do with your availability. Is this the direction I should be going? Should I be spending my time here? Is this what I should be doing now?

INVEST YOUR TIME WISELY

"As much as I want to, I can't right now." So how should you invest your time and your limited resources?

The answer depends on the type of return you want when you invest your time, when you invest your availability. What is it that you are seeking from God? A breakthrough in prayer? A breakthrough in His Word? A breakthrough in a struggle? Whatever it is you are seeking, you must make sure you are available to God to receive it.

Not only must you be available physically, but you must also be available in heart, mind, and spirit. You need to make time to speak to God in prayer and allow Him to speak to you through His Word. As you yield this time to prayer, expect God to reveal to you what is needed for you to move forward. This becomes a time of affirmation, a time when God can affirm your present. Without it you can't move forward with confidence.

AFFIRM YOUR PRESENT

The result of affirmation is confirmation. It means that you are already speaking in the past tense about what is still in process. Too often we wait to see what God is going to do and if it will work out. Yet if God told you something, you can believe it and live accordingly. The only thing you are waiting for is for it to come to pass. You won't be surprised—you'll be affirmed.

4

Acquire Missing/Necessary Resources: Fulfill Your Vision/Destiny

The prophet helped the widow woman affirm her present condition. She may have thought she had only "a little oil," but with his help she realized she had much more: her two sons. The creditors recognized their value because they sought to make them indentured servants. She was oblivious to their worth because she had been overwhelmed by her own grief and desperation.

During the course of their brief conversation, however, the prophet could discern what was needed for her to achieve her goals. With this knowledge he could properly advise her on what to do, where to go, who could help.

One of the things she failed to realize is that others around her—her sons, her neighbors— could help. Other than her own pot of oil, which in that day was a valued commodity, she lacked the containers or at least didn't have enough of them for what was about to happen. The prophet helped her realize this when he told her in 2 Kings 4:3, *"Go, borrow thee vessels abroad of all thy neighbours, even empty vessels; borrow not a few."*

Sometimes during a crisis moment or when pressed for a solution to a problem, we can overlook the people around us, especially those in our own house. Once she understood that her sons could benefit the family, she was prepared to take the next step.

THE POWER OF PEOPLE

People are an appreciable asset much like any asset that may gain value over time. People and the synergy they create will benefit any organization.

Once she realized how her sons and neighbors could assist her, she was prepared to take the next step. It was time to move from a state of grief and loss into her purpose. In order to advance her purpose, she needed to acquire the necessary resources. She needed to close the gap between what she had and what she needed.

Although we don't know her relationship with her neighbors, the prophet's advice brought to bear the possibilities of building healthy relationships that come back to bless us when we need them most. The value of other people around us in our lives can be the missing link as to whether or not we survive or thrive. Like the widow woman, you may need to take the risk and reach out to others who may have the skills, resources, and expertise you need. Take the risk and inquire about—

- OPM: other people's money

- OPS: other people's skills

- OPK: other people's knowledge

- OPE: other people's equipment

The result of her risk-taking is that other people cared enough and were willing to help her, which proved to be a significant turning point. It is powerful after seeking assistance to then discover, "I'm not as alone now. People do care."

It can be a powerful moment to discover that maybe what I really need in my life is enough top-quality relationships. And when it matters the most, other people can help fill in the gaps with their equipment, money, skills, and knowledge—just as the prophet, unencumbered with the widow's burden, is able to show her how to become her own solution to her crisis.

It is important to note that she took responsibility for her situation. This is so critical when you find yourself needing the aid of other people—that you don't ask other people to take on the responsibility of your life and future. If you are able to define where you are going and seek the assistance of people you know have necessary pieces to your puzzle, it can be the reason that people are willing to help you grow and go to the next level. No one person can know, be skilled at, and possess all the needed resources to achieve his or her goals and dreams.

CONSIDER A COACH

It is important in the process of going anywhere that you take the time to review where you are and determine whether you have all that you need to arrive and to arrive on time.

In reality the widow woman needed a coaching relationship with the prophet to know that she required a lot of vessels. By asking her neighbors for help, she could not limit her belief to just a small amount of vessels. The prophet-turned-success-coach positioned her for a huge win by telling her, *"Borrow thee vessels abroad of all thy neighbours, even empty vessels; borrow not a few."*

It is not uncommon when asking for help to minimize the need by stating, "Anything you can do to help would make a huge difference." Although we can all relate to the sentiment of not wanting to burden someone else with our troubles, the prophet encouraged the widow woman to expect a huge return on her investment and to realize that she had to be prepared to handle what was about to happen through her efforts and those of her sons.

People are the greatest appreciable asset and when given proper training, they increase in untold value over time to meet the present and future needs of an organization. This also is true of families, churches, leaders, and others.

J. Paul Getty once said, "I'd rather have one percent of the effort of 100 men than 100 percent of my own effort."

Like the widow woman, you may be learning the truth of this statement, that many successful people don't rely on simply their own efforts to achieve their destinies—they acquire and use all necessary resources for their benefit.

When you begin with a definite purpose, it becomes the primary tool in determining what's missing, what else is needed to get ahead. You must value the efforts and resources of others by including them with mutual benefit. Because the widow woman borrowed the needed vessels and was projected to make a profit from their help, it was reasonable to expect that there would be some sort of return for the lender.

Although her husband's debt was the reason for her predicament, she was advised to borrow to gain the hope of getting out of this situation.

On the surface, this advice can appear suspect; however, the advice she received had an expectation of more than enough in return, which made borrowing a necessary risk that many might consider and even engage in as a normal course of business.

The widow woman's case reveals that you must properly value what you have and demonstrate your belief by taking appropriate risks to achieve the desired end. It is equally important to develop trusted relationships with those who give you advice in order to avoid situations in which the advice comes only to enhance the self-interest of those giving it.

This is all part of your plan to take your current value and acquire additional resources as necessary and create the future that is yours.

5

Assemble Everything into a Workable Plan: Create a Plan and Work Environment in Which Your Plan Will Work

Principle number 5 is to assemble everything into a workable plan. In 2 Kings 4:5 we read, *So she went from him and shut the door behind her and her sons, who brought the vessels to her; and she poured it out* (NKJV).

Plans are tricky. Sometimes they can be presented in a great document but are impractical. In this principle we focus on creating the plan and the work environment so that the plan is successful. It is one thing to have a good plan, but if you lack the proper work environment, you can live unfulfilled with a good plan. The environments in which things happen are just as important as the plan itself. They are critical to each other.

As we continue with these principles, remember to check the house on a regular basis. It cannot be a one-time thing. The house itself is a tremendous asset. When you make it a practice to reassess your plan, you will find new meaning, new assets, and new discoveries in the house.

The widow woman is now in a position to develop a plan and make it a real part of her future. With the pot of oil handy, she did as the prophet directed her to do. She and her sons borrowed as many empty vessels as they could from neighbors and were now ready to set up shop.

Up to this point the widow woman had completed all the proper steps:

- She assessed her situation by checking her house.

- She appraised what she had in her house and what she and her sons had gathered.

- She made an assessment to determine the true value of what she possessed.

- She evaluated everything with a critical eye to develop her own opinion and to gain a sense of confidence.

- She affirmed her present by examining what she had available and made sure she and her sons were available to put their resources to good use.

- She acquired the missing albeit necessary resources to move forward.

Have you taken the time to assess, appraise, affirm, and acquire? Are you checking your house to be sure you haven't overlooked something that may prove beneficial to your plan? Have you taken the time to critically analyze your plan to be sure you have covered all the key issues and are confident enough to move forward? After all, your opinion matters, as it will also affect how other people view your plan. If you have doubts, so will others. If you act as if your plan is not worth a lot of attention, others will discount it too.

RIGHT TIME

As you put your plan together, you might feel as if you should have done it years ago. Information and the process may not come easily. Times and processes have changed. Technology has brought our world closer. You may have to work harder than you anticipated to gather all your resources.

Even if you think you lost time, remember who you are dealing with. Remember who you have committed this plan to. God is the creator of time, which means that any-time He wants to make up time, He can. God is not limit-ed by time so He can fast-forward you and not miss a beat.

VALUE THE VALUABLE

The widow woman realized the value of her sons. The fact that the creditor vowed to take them if she was unable to pay the debt was enough for her to acknowledge their worth and decide how they could be used. Notice that her crisis had become their crisis, giving her more to work with.

She also realized the value of the prophet. While we don't know for certain, we can infer that the woman's husband spent his life serving God and was connected to prophets like Elisha. It made sense that she would seek the prophet's help. After all, as she reminded the prophet, *"Thou knowest that thy servant did fear the Lord"* (2 Kings 4:1). His legacy of faith may have influenced her enough to seek out the prophet's advice and guidance.

After following the prophet's instructions, the scripture tells us that *She went from him and shut the door behind her and her sons* (2 Kings 4:5 NKJV)—suggesting that she needed to pause and reflect on her situation and the next steps she planned to take.

Since her circumstances also involved her sons, she had to figure out how this plan was going to work. She used this opportunity to innovate. She needed to ask the tough questions: *How can I do this? Who else can help me? What might this cost me in terms of time and money? Am I available?*

If you don't use this time wisely, you might talk yourself out of your plan because you haven't explored the different issues and obstacles that may arise or how you might handle them. Plans and ideas may come to you at a busy time in your life, rendering you unable to pause or give them proper consideration. You may feel like abandoning your plan, but don't—pause.

It is important to take time to pause, to avail yourself to a time of reflection so you can determine the true value of the plan, the idea, and the experience and then figure out the appropriate action.

She assembled a plan of action that involved her sons, the pot of oil, the empty vessels, and her house.

CREATE A PLAN

The widow woman had the prophet and her sons as part of her plan. Yet other elements of her plan were more important: God, faith, and the right environment to nourish the plan.

The moment she began gathering the empty vessels demonstrated her faith in God. Her faith was not in the oil but in what God could do with it. Though not yet realized, God was going to make the oil more than enough to satisfy what she needed.

Faith is essential to the success of any plan. In Hebrews 11:6 we are told, *Without faith it is impossible to please him: for he that cometh to God must believe that he is, and that he is a rewarder of them that diligently seek him.*

It is better to take a risk believing God because when you step out on God's Word, it isn't really a risk; rather, it is just the pressure that our human frailty experiences in order to get to it.

You cannot achieve a plan without faith. Faith has to be part of the plan.

As you create your plan, understand that you will struggle. This is a step where you get to learn how to do what you eventually want to do because the best of you will come alive. It is part of the process that you need to experience so that regardless of the challenges you encounter, your faith remains intact and will see you through. If you don't experience the struggle, you'll never understand who you are or what you are capable of accomplishing.

Use this time to learn what you need to learn, gain what you need to gain, develop what you need to develop. All plans require a type of waiting period or struggle so that when the time is right and opportunities arise, you will be prepared to seize them. If you are unprepared the opportunity will be lost.

LOCATION. LOCATION. LOCATION.

Your plan should also include a good work environment. When starting a business, it is imperative that you consider the location. For example, if you were to open a Mexican restaurant in a Hispanic community, the residents would come because the business matches the community. The environment matches what you are seeking to do and will cause somebody to take notice. Should the business not match what the community needs, you can expect to have difficulties because the environment is wrong.

For the widow woman and her sons, the best location proved to be their house. The work environment was critical to their success. The house is where all the activity took place—from determining the value of the oil to filling the empty vessels.

In essence, they were able to create a home-based business. Everything they produced took place in the home. Not only did they have the ability to produce what could be exchanged, but they also had the ability to sell and negotiate it.

Remember Your Plan, Your Purpose

As you pursue your plan, make sure your priorities are in order. A sure way to do this is to be available in the presence of God. You will become mission centered. Your life will be fulfilling God's purpose through the work you do rather than by trying to fit God into your life and your work.

6

Attach to the Purpose/Plan:
Be Committed to the Mission

What does it mean to be *attached* to something? *Attached* by definition refers to "being committed, devoted, bound to, faithful to." The word requires some action, and as we explore this principle, we want to explore what it means to be committed, to be attached to or devoted to something.

One of the concepts related to being attached to the mission is commitment, which means to be dedicated to a call, activity, or job. It's rooted in our intellectual as well as emotional being. Commitment reminds us why we do certain things, why we are involved in certain things, why we go certain places. Commitment requires us to focus on things in the right way.

In principle 5 we explored assembling everything together to create a workable plan and then create a work environment that outlined the vision, how we would work together, and the process for getting the work done.

A person can be excited about his or her job because of the environment but if that same person is not committed to the job, the excitement will wear off over time. Life situations will cause the person to ask, "Why should I get up and go there anymore? Why should I keep going in that direction?" It's only a matter of time before he or she begins to experience an emotional season that potentially jeopardizes long-term success, especially if there's no commitment.

The widow had come a long way since the death of her spouse. She had a good plan and her sons were willing to help her execute her plan so as to rebuild their lives. Yet she still had some things to work out.

Like the widow, you can't be on your way to a great future without a great plan. You can do all the right things, consult the right people, develop your necessary resources. You can do all these things to create a great plan—and be committed to none of it.

A plan without action is just a plan.

This is why it is important to attach yourself, to commit yourself to what you are trying to accomplish.

BE COMMITTED

As we explore 2 Kings 4:5, we see that the widow and her sons went inside their house, shut the door, and immediately went to work: *So she went from him [the prophet], and shut the door upon her and upon her sons, who brought the vessels to her; and she poured out.*

The family went to work.

Some people sit around and talk about their plan and maybe do a little of the work—but it never gets off the ground, and a year later they are still talking about their plan. Not so with the widow woman.

Her decision to do what the prophet advised demonstrated her resolve, her willingness to commit to something greater than her grief, greater than her loss. "She poured out"—this lets us know that she gave her all; she withheld nothing. Similarly, if we want to move forward with our plans, we too must not go about it half-hearted. We must be committed. We must attach ourselves to the mission.

When you attach yourself, you will become so intertwined with your mission that it becomes you and you become it. You cannot imagine not doing this. You cannot imagine being separated from it. Even on a bad day you realize that you must do what you must do because you are committed to the mission. This commitment will compel you to do your part even if others fall short, forget, and disengage.

Even when you cannot see the end result or fully understand how things are supposed to evolve, you know that if God is part of the plan, it is a sure thing.

As David reminds us in Psalm 37:25, *I have been young, and now am old; yet have I not seen the righteous forsaken, nor his seed begging bread.* God will not leave us without a solution or leave a question unanswered. The prophet gave her an answer and she followed through. In sum, she borrowed as many empty vessels as she could from her neighbors, she and her sons returned home, she shut the door, and she poured out.

Remember: she began with just a little oil. We don't know how many vessels (jars) she borrowed or their size. All we know is that she poured—into jar after jar after jar. Imagine her excitement seeing the "little oil" replenished time and again. It didn't take long for her to become fully committed, to become attached to the one job she had: to pour out.

This also demonstrates how you too, regardless of your circumstances, must be committed. You may start off small, not seeing immediate results and not feeling or even believing that you are making progress. The key is to remain committed, particularly if you have prayed and asked God for guidance.

This kind of commitment commands focus. And with this focus you must be dedicated to the outcome. You cannot be worried about the cost of the mission; rather, you must be focused on the mission itself, what it is you are trying to accomplish, the plan you seek to bring forth.

If we pay too much attention to the cost, we can easily lose our focus, especially if the results are not coming as quickly as we might like. You might feel that the effort you are putting in is not worth the cost and you therefore no longer want to do it.

This is a familiar scenario. People want to be successful but don't necessarily want to put in the time and effort to be successful. They want to look the part, to appear successful, but not do the work in order to sustain the part—success.

It's much like our relationship with God. You must first give yourself over completely to God; yield your ways to His ways. Like Jesus, who sacrificed Himself for all humanity, we must also freely give ourselves over to God in order to have a solid relationship with Him. It requires a total commitment, which means that since God says to repent, to turn away from and give up sin, then that is what you must do.

If you think it is too much, you will jeopardize your relationship. You have to ask yourself, "Is it worth the cost? Is it worth my commitment?"

You can't have a meaningful mission in God without God. The only real deed God wants us to do is give our lives to Him. That requires commitment. And the widow's commitment to God, to her mission, had everything to do with her success. Her attitude also played a key role. It represented her emotional attachment to the mission.

7

Aware of Opportunities/Seasons: Understand the Window of Opportunity You Are Afforded

Understand the season, the window of opportunity you are afforded, and maximize the moment.

You've decided to move forward with your plan. You've made a commitment that no matter what, no matter how difficult things may become, no matter how slow and incremental the progress is, you will continue to do whatever is required for your plan to materialize.

This kind of mind-set or attitude is necessary in order to remain focused on your plan.

So what's next?

In addition to your commitment and a positive attitude, you also need to be ready to seize the opportunity when it comes.

Ecclesiastes 3:1 reminds us that *to every thing there is a season, and a time to every purpose under the heaven.*

The opportunity will come in the right season. The challenge is to be able to identify the season you are experiencing.

Expect seasons in your life that address different issues you are encountering. You may be in a season of drought or lack, when nothing seems to go right, when you seemingly don't have enough to get by. Funds and other resources never quite cover all your needs. Or perhaps you are facing a spiritual drought, feeling that your prayers are not being heard or that you are unable to hear God's voice.

You might also experience a season of struggle, when you can't seem to go far enough or advance fast enough in your career, your education, or your business.

Maybe the season you are in is one of blessings. You sought God for something specific, a one-time thing, and He showed you favor. You received what it was you asked of Him.

If you are continuing in your mission and pursuing your purpose, expect at some point to enter a season of more than enough, a season when you have an overflow that you may not know how to handle. We often know how to be resourceful when we have too little. But what about when we have an overflow? How do you deal with more than enough? Where do you put it? Do you share it? Is there a bank or credit union large enough to handle this overflow?

This is the season that the widow woman experienced: a season of more than enough.

How did she get here? How was she able to recognize this season in her life?

IDENTIFY THE SEASON

Throughout her grief she remained prayerful. She took care of her sons. Although Scripture does not explicitly say that this woman was religious or followed the religion or teachings of her husband, we do know that she had a little faith and that she knew enough to seek help and guidance from the prophet.

In 2 Kings 4:6 we are told simply, *So the oil ceased* (NKJV).

This leads to the seventh principle: Be aware of the window of opportunity or the season.

To do so, you must be in the present. You have to learn to live in a state of awareness because some things come and go so fast that by the time you recognize that it was of God, the words of affirmation you were waiting for might be gone.

It is important for you to be aware of every opportunity God has placed before you because you need to move and move with timing because some things happen only in their season. If you miss that season, however, it doesn't mean that it won't come around again.

For example, certain flowers bloom only in the spring. By the summer they are gone. No amount of tilling, watering, and fertilizing will bring them back. They are gone—until next spring.

Thus, it is important for you to be aware, to be fully present so you can be sensitive to the spirit of God.

"The oil ceased" presented a window of opportunity that was afforded this particular woman. She needed what one might term a "right-now miracle," a "right-now breakthrough," in part because of the desperate financial situation she and her family were in.

How would you respond if you knew there was a miracle in your house? You would definitely pay attention to everything. It would make you investigate, to look at things in your house that you ordinarily would not look at or pay attention to because you pass by them every day. *Haven't I seen this before? Hasn't it been on the shelf for some time now?*

If you pay close attention you'll rediscover some things that have been in your house *the whole time.* Now is the season to use them.

THE SEASON TO GROW

In your state of awareness and readiness, you also might experience a season of temptation, in which God is trying to prove you through a process to be sure you will stick with the mission, stick with the role and the vision

He has laid out. During this season He allows things to come to pass that will either bring the best out of you—or the worst.

This season cannot be avoided. The whole point is to purge the worst out of you so that you deal with it. We may have issues and problems in our lives that we have concealed, that are under the surface and are preventing us from going to the next level.

You won't be able to progress until the underlying issues are resolved. God wants to help you gain the confidence you need to handle the "more than enough" that is soon to unfold.

The widow woman—and anyone else in similar dire straits with few resources, few transferrable skills, little family or community support—had little faith, if any, from which to draw. It's often said that faith isn't faith until one has been through challenging times. Too often our faith is really just talk because we haven't experienced or had a specific area in our life tested. Instead, we exhibit determination. Although determination is a good trait to have, you need to increase your faith. And your faith won't become genuine until you've been through a few difficult and challenging seasons.

Certainly you might fail or come up short. But don't give up. Instead, get up and press on, asking God to renew your strength, your resolve, your commitment.

God will allow certain temptations in our lives—not to see us fail but to make us the real deal. Temptation is rooted in adversity, affliction, and trouble. When your strength fails in the day of adversity, that means your strength is small (Proverbs 24:10). God will not allow any hardship on you beyond what He knows you can handle. In fact, He already knows how you are going to get through it.

This season of temptation is commonplace—it is not unique to you. He's trying to fortify you and strengthen your character. In fact, for every temptation that comes your way, for every adverse situation you face, for every affliction that comes upon you, for every trial you experience—God has already made a way of escape.

> *There hath no temptation taken you but such as is common to man: but God is faithful, who will not suffer you to be tempted above that ye are able; but will with the temptation also make a way to escape, that ye may be able to bear it.*
> (1 Corinthians 10:13)

This is why you must be aware. You must be sensitive and ready to move when God says it's time to move to get out of difficult situations or avoid trouble. Otherwise you may find yourself mired in a predicament longer than you need to be.

Some of our failures occur because we didn't respond or

move when God moved. We were unaware. We were doing things our way and we missed out on what God needed to share with us.

God wants us to succeed.

To every thing there is a season and a time to every purpose under the heaven. Everything has a purpose under the sun. When a season is over, it's over. The goal is to remain aware so that you can respond in season and seize the moment, to take advantage of the opportunities that are presented to you.

Keep in mind, however, that you may not get all the details or answers. Sometimes you just have to be ready. Remember: God is in control. Once God has declared it, no demon in hell will be able to alter, interrupt, interfere, or halt what He has ordained for you. It is going to happen as He intended.

The widow and her sons did as the prophet said: Beginning with that one jar of oil, they went throughout the community and gathered as many vessels as they could. They returned to their home, shut the door, and began pouring oil into each vessel. At some point one of her sons told her, *"There is not another vessel." So the oil ceased* (2 Kings 4:6 NKJV).

They had reached their capacity.

By following the instructions of the prophet, the woman and her sons seized the moment and maximized the time they had. Their commitment, awareness, and readiness produced much more than they ever imagined. They ran out of vessels—not oil.

When God releases your abundance, don't reduce your vision or your faith, causing Him to withhold all He has for you. Remember: you must be aware of both the season and the moment.

8

Apply Yourself:
Exchange the Finished Product for Full Value

Exchange is a mutual benefit proposition; therefore it is important to know what you have. It is equally important to know the value, as well as the cost associated with what you bring to the table to exchange. Destiny does not come with a discount, so whatever you achieve, produce, and/or offer as an exchangeable product or service has its own unique costs. It is up to you to determine the fair exchange value with those who want, need, and are willing to pay for what you have to offer.

To know what you have is to consider the purpose that it would serve for other people and/or organizations. This critical piece of information is a tremendous help in how you communicate the value of your product and/or service and what you are willing to negotiate with others in mutual benefit exchange. One of the greatest challenges in this process is finding and getting it into the hands of those who know what its value would mean to them and want it enough to pay for it.

A major part of this process is knowing your target audience or, said another way, who your customers are. Where are they located? How do I connect with them? This was something the widow had to learn about quickly. Once she and her sons filled all the empty vessels with oil, she went to get further instruction from the prophet-turned-success-coach:

> *And it came to pass, when the vessels were full, that she said unto her son, Bring me yet a vessel. And he said unto her, There is not a vessel more. And the oil stayed. Then she came and told the man of God. And he said, Go, sell the oil, and pay thy debt, and live thou and thy children of the rest.*
> (2 Kings 4:6–7)

Simply put, he told her, "Go, sell the oil." In other words, go find who wants, needs, and is willing to exchange value for value. And with that, create enough means to satisfy your old debt as well as the additional debt that you took on to produce the value to others.

His instruction was the push she needed to create a legitimate business venture. She now had something of value that she and her sons produced together as a family business. The stakeholder pool had increased as well,

which automatically factored into the exchange value needed to satisfy the requirements of the business and all its
stakeholders.

Maybe there is an ideal solution that meets the needs
of others that will enable you to entertain the possibility of
generating income. It is vitally important to apply yourself
to your chosen field of endeavor. As leadership expert and
author John Maxwell teaches in *The Law of the Lid,* everything rises and falls on leadership. Whether you are the formal leader in your environment or the greatest influencer,
you determine how far your organization can go. With the
prophet's encouragement, the widow woman committed
and applied herself to her plan to use the oil-filled vessels to
her good. Although the scripture doesn't indicate, we can
have the confidence that she paid her debts and generated
sufficient profits to "live thou and thy children of the rest."

9

Attend to Your Needs:
Satisfy Personal Needs

It's easy to get caught up in the busyness of life to the point that you neglect yourself, not taking care of yourself in the ways you should: getting proper rest, eating a balanced diet, getting exercise, having quiet times, nurturing relationships.

You set and pursue goals, work overtime, and do various things to get ahead. And sometimes if you are not careful, the person who gets neglected is *you*. When you neglect to take care of yourself, you're prone to quit, to abandon your goals and purpose.

It doesn't matter what your title is, how important you think you are, whether you wear a suit to work every day or drive a truck across town—self-care is essential.

As we continue to explore the widow in 2 Kings 4:1–7, we are reminded of her plight. She is a woman in crisis, but she is not in crisis by herself. She has two sons, but following the death of her husband she's had to become the head of the household. She's had to navigate the course as well as follow the instructions of the prophet to go.

But where? And to do what?

If you move aimlessly and without purpose, you'll soon become worn out, tired, mean, and irritable—because you can't go without purpose too far for too long. You'll become frustrated with yourself because you'll be unable to answer these basic questions: *Why? Why am I doing this? What is this all about?* However, if you can answer the simple question *Why?* then you're moving in the right direction.

To reach the next step you must do the proper due diligence or you won't understand what's required. You won't be in a position to make proper decisions, connect with the right people, or move forward with your plans. The widow woman had to learn her own value and that there was value in the oil she possessed.

Once you recognize your own value, your own worth, you can exchange that value for something else of value. Other people will realize your worth and seek you out. You'll also understand that you have every right to attend to your needs. You'll understand the importance of "me time" and the need for self-care.

TYPES OF DEBT | ATTEND TO YOUR NEEDS

The prophet told the woman to pay her debts. However, we will refer to it as the widow attending to her needs

DISCOVER the MIRACLE in YOUR HOUSE

because that is what created the crisis in the first place. Everything that was secure and stable was jeopardized because of the debt she owed. When you neglect yourself, when you fail to attend to your needs—your debts—you become subject to someone else.

The prophet authorized her to pay her debt as part of the solution for her life. After all, she came to the prophet and God for a solution to a traumatic life situation. With two sons to raise and no one to support them, it was imperative that she take care of herself, which meant to pay her husband's debt. Possibly her husband had not had a financial needs analysis (FNA), which would have helped him know what he needed to secure the long-term future of his family in the event of his untimely death. The FNA positions you to create an immediate estate. Go to http://www.primerica.com/PBCT3 and make an appointment to secure your family's long-term future now.

It is hard to get beyond debt. We can't live without it. You will always owe someone something in exchange for the value of what you want. Some debt is normal, such as paying a utility company to provide heat to your home. Other debt may be the result of wants—a new laptop computer, a new vehicle, a Mediterranean cruise—but you don't have the resources.

We have to be careful not to become so financially imperiled that we spend most of our lives in financial debt to the point that God takes a back seat. Just as you invest in your home, your education, charitable organizations, IRAs, and bonds, God wants us to invest in the kingdom. He wants us to invest in ourselves. He doesn't want us to tell Him, "But God, I've got these bills to pay—You understand."

Avoid having to choose between God and debt. Avoid having to negotiate with God and missing out on His intentional blessings. First Corinthians 6:19–20 reminds us that we are accountable to God: *Know ye not that your body is the temple of the Holy Ghost which is in you, which ye have of God, and ye are not your own? For ye are bought with a price: therefore glorify God in your body, and in your spirit, which are God's.*

Excessive Burden

Debt is not always financial. It also can be defined as overextending yourself or even over-leveraging yourself. In either case, you are doing much more than you are mentally and physically, perhaps even spiritually, capable of doing. In sum, you are trying to do too much in a short space of time.

This may occur when you fail to establish priorities, when you overcommit, or when you multitask, mistakenly believing that you can do it all if you do a little of each task until all are completed. You can become so busy doing so many different things that you are still unavailable to pay your first debt, which is to God.

At some point you may want to relieve yourself of the excessive burden type of debt. Self-discipline, recognizing your limitations, and simply saying no are key. You must apply this principle—attending to your needs—in order to serve God freely, in order to serve Him in the way He wants to be served.

GRATITUDE

Debt also can be ascribed to a feeling of gratitude. A service or favor puts a new twist on the idea of debt. When debt is associated with gratitude, it usually involves a person: someone did something great or was generous to us and we feel indebted to him or her. You may even reply, "I owe you one."

Those who are honest about it are looking for an opportunity to return the kindness in some way. Sometimes the best way to return a favor is to succeed rather than to go back and ask for another favor.

The feeling of gratitude places you inwardly in a place of being in debt.

WHO YOU REALLY OWE

As mentioned previously, our first debt is to God.

Jesus paid the ultimate price with His life. He paid the debt for our sin, our sinful nature, our natural disobedience. His payment put each of us in a position to have a relationship with God.

It is not just monetary though there is a monetary component in that we are instructed in Malachi 3:10 to *bring ye all the tithes into the storehouse, that there may be meat in mine house.* In other words, our giving ensures that the work of the church toward kingdom-building is fulfilled.

Unlike the IRS, the mortgage company, or the student loan agency, God does not force us to give. He will not garnish our wages, issue a fine, or impose a higher rate of interest. Instead, He trusts that we will do as He has instructed.

When you place God first, when you honor debt to Him first, you can be assured that He will provide. You may even begin to feel a sense of gratitude toward God, wishing you had more to give Him for the favor He has given you.

Yet the best way to repay God is through praise. Praise is suitable for anyone at any time and anywhere that you ponder where He has brought you from and the ways He has brought you through. Praise is a reasonable action considering the debt that was paid on our behalf.

When you get to the point where gratitude to God is a natural part of your life, it will be on display. You live in a state of praise. Your gratitude becomes your attitude.

FINAL PAYMENT

The widow did as the prophet instructed. She created something of value that benefited not only her family but also others who recognized her value and that of the oil she possessed. She was now in a position to exchange value for value. She had more than enough to pay her husband's debts.

The prophet's message applied also to her. Satisfying the debt meant she must also attend to her own needs. She could not overcommit, overextend, or over-leverage herself. Rather, he was reminding her that once she had done well for herself, she "owed" it to herself to take care of herself and her sons, as they were instrumental in her success. She could now take care of her family over a sustained period. She no longer had to consider how she would make it through the day. Her future was solid.

She did not produce by herself those vessels filled with oil. With the help of her neighbors who lent her the vessels and the assistance of her sons, who helped to fill them, she produced more than enough. In doing so, she met her obligations to God and her obligation to her creditors. Now it was time for her to honor those who helped make it possible.

As you move toward fulfilling your purpose and goals, you cannot forget those who provided advice, resources, guidance, expertise, even instructions on the best course of action. It's important that you honor them, as they were essential to helping you move forward.

10

Advance Your Life:
Plan a Sustainable Life with the
Overflow/Profit

Plan a sustainable life (having done the will of God) with the overflow/profit.

Success is good, but you have to keep it in balance and celebrate God in all the success. You never need to elevate yourself, because it comes with the progress in the process.

You may be in a season when you don't feel like celebrating God but you celebrate Him anyway. You may have hit rock bottom yet continue to celebrate while others are asking, *Why me?* or calling it quits. But as you learn to dance in the darkness, you can move on to the next season.

Remember, however, that you can't get anywhere without a process. You must get used to process in your life and the idea that process takes time.

If you try to cut corners, it only means you are going through a different process. You cannot cheat process, but you can, however, choose which process you go through and what that process might look like.

It may be as simple as changing your attitude about the situation, the circumstance, or the person because the process is going to take place regardless of how you feel about it.

This leads us to the tenth principle of a breakthrough life: You need to advance your life, and always with the caveat: having done the will of God. But you can't advance your life beyond the will of God. Life is best lived *within* the will of God because it becomes the safest place on the planet. Even when danger lurks and deadly things are around—in the will of God you remain safe.

There will come a point when you go through the process that the only thing left is to advance your life.

As we return to 2 Kings 4, let's be reminded of the last three assignments required of the widow woman. The prophet first told her to go and sell the oil. Second, he told her to pay the debt. The third and final assignment was "You and your sons live."

She went and told the man of God, and he said, "Go, sell the oil and pay your debts. You and your sons can live on what is left" (NIV).

Part of God's direction to us is to live. One would think that we wouldn't have to be told to live. But sometimes we do because we get caught up in the moment; we get caught up in the stress. We get caught up in the pressure of what's going on around us and we forget to live in the process.

In this tenth principle God tells us to live. It's already been clearly established that you don't live outside the will of God—you live in God and God lives in you. When you think about the Christian life, it is that God is living through us, which simply means that all we have to do is agree to go along with the journey.

Jesus had to come to grips with this Himself, and it was played out in the Garden of Gethsemane in Matthew 26. The garden encounter served as a wrestling of the wills. The human will and the divine will are engaged in a wrestling match, a tug of war, and both were wanting to dominate Jesus's life.

By the third time of wrestling wills, Jesus came to the conclusion: "*O my Father, if it be possible, let this cup pass from me: nevertheless not as I will, but as thou wilt*" (Matthew 26:39).

Difficult or not, we too must get to the point at which we're willing to live out our purposes. In essence, *Whatever Your will is for me, Lord, count me in. I'm all in. I'm going with You, Lord. I may not understand all of it, but nevertheless, not my will but Yours be done.*

Everyone has to come to that place. The widow woman. Jesus. You.

And in that process, you must make the decision to live—not your will but God's will. Everything you need is encompassed in His will far beyond what you can imagine or think. You may feel as if you have to give up something, that you have to give up life to choose God. But you don't really get to live until you choose God. Why? You are giving up sin, which destroys life, and you get God, who gives life. You make His will your highest priority. You are simply offering to God your reasonable service, which means that anything else is unreasonable.

The prophet says in very clear terms to her, "You and your sons—live." Under pressure? Live. Under stress? Live. Have too little? Live. Trying to decide what to do with so much? Live. Anytime we encounter similar circumstances, as the prophet admonished the widow woman, we too must *live.*

A TIME TO GROW

Let's examine what it means to live. According to the Oxford Dictionary, *life* is the period between the birth and death of a living thing, especially a human being. It also means the ability to grow, the ability to change.

The ability to grow gives us the context for the dash between the two dates, called birth and death, the beginning and end of human life.

In between, God gives us the ability to grow. When you decide to live and really engage in life, then you begin the process of growing. This can involve physical, mental, intellectual, emotional, and even financial growth. The prophet is telling the woman that he wants her and her sons to grow. They have been through a lot already, but now, for the rest of your life, he tells them, I want you to live.

TO BE

Another form of *live* is *to be*. Sometimes in our doing, in our busyness, we take on a "doing" mind-set that if we are not doing anything then we are not living. Some may say that if you are not having fun (or sinning), you are not living. When asked, "What do you do for fun?" it's often a guide to find out what your vices are. But to live is to be.

Too often when we get into the mode of living, it is in comparison to someone else—whether you have the same amount or less, whether you are achieving more than the next person or are achieving less. You measure yourself against others' standards when it's better instead to be what God called you to be. God made you who you are and it's okay to be you.

TO CONTINUE

To live is to continue to grow. You cannot get stuck and stop. You must continue, which means it is not about how fast and how far you go. *To live* means you have to be in present possession of things. The opposite of this is to always be in want. The Scripture has already made it clear in Psalm 23 that *The Lord is my shepherd; I shall not want.* Realize that God is taking care of you, making sure that you have what you need. This means that you can live in the moment and to have, whether it is too little or too much.

The danger is when we begin measuring ourselves against someone else who we think has more. While this person may have more material things, he or she may not have more peace. You can rest at night but the other person has no peace because he or she is on guard duty trying to make sure no one comes along to steal. The key here is to learn to be content in whatever state you are in, because any day in God is a good day—it's God who makes the difference.

TO MAINTAIN

To live is to maintain. You are making sure that you keep some things constant, stable, and solid in your life. You maintain good spiritual discipline by reading the Word and praying daily, because as Jesus said in Matthew 4:4, *"Man shall not live by bread alone, but by every word that proceedeth out of the mouth of God."* So to maintain, you need the Word of God every day of your life. Whether it is a verse, a chapter—it does not matter. But every day you need the Word of God in order to live.

People who are content with living are not externally defining life. Rather, they are internally defining life. If it has to come from outside of you for you to live, you'll always be waiting for something to come or something to happen before you can start living.

Should someone find out that you need a particular thing, he or she can withhold life from you to manipulate you. Yet when you live despite everything else and everyone else's opinions, then guess what—people are still going to have opinions. Don't allow yourself to get worked up over others' opinions. If you learn to be content, you can enjoy life.

TO OCCUPY

To live also means to occupy. This means you have to be industrious about yourself, doing the things that are consistent with why you are here. When you are young, your main occupation is that of a student. In a short period in your life, you must learn all that you can and then apply yourself to doing it. Treat it—being a student—like a job. You desire to do well and if you do, your work as a student will reap benefits because you did your job.

It also is important that you occupy the God space, the divine moments in your life. Everyone has them as our natural lives evolve from occupying our divine place. Matthew 6:33 confirms this when Jesus says, *"Seek first his kingdom and his righteousness, and all these things will be given to you as well"* (NIV). This comes out of divine purpose. It is part of the benefit package demonstrating that if you do the will of God, the will of God will take care of you.

TO EXPERIENCE

You cannot experience life being scared. You cannot sit on the sidelines. You cannot live your life being afraid of everything and everybody. Part of the experience is trying new things. And when you approach this with godly intentions, godly motives, and a godly heart, you have more freedom to live.

But when you live in sin, you are always on pins and needles. The Bible in Proverbs 13:15 says, *Good understanding giveth favour: but the way of transgressors is hard.* Not so with the believer. The believer's life is more at ease because not only do you get the freedom to live, but you also get a divine Protector who will shield you from some bad stuff.

Understand this about life: no one gets out alive. So try a few new things, even if it looks as if it is going to cost you. *New,* however, does not mean *foolish.* It simply means not to let fear or lack of understanding prevent you from trying something new and different.

Experience is a part of living. There will come a time when you need to give that life away—share your experiences—with others. You want to get to heaven with a life on empty, a life well lived.

The journey of the widow was all about learning how to go from nothing to abundance. That is the whole miracle of the house. She was learning how to live with nothing and moving in hope toward more than she could imagine. In the process she learned how to apply herself, occupy, try new things, take some risks, and have faith.

TO GAIN ETERNAL LIFE: ABUNDANCE

Ideally you should be living in such a way that you can live again—that is, live with God in eternity. This simply means that living for God now sets you up to live with Him in eternity.

When the widow woman heard the instruction "You and your sons live," it was a call to her to live in a certain manner. Like this woman, you could own your own business; or get several promotions, earn PhDs, and receive honorary doctorates. These are great achievements, but they are temporary, limiting your abundance only to this life.

God offers true and complete abundance through our relationship with Him through Jesus Christ. Choose that relationship with Him today (John 3:5, 3:16; Acts 2:38; Titus 3:5)!

Living the Principles

Early in our marriage and ministry we learned that our combined education, experience, and empowerment from the Holy Spirit were a miraculous synergy. Joseph, a naturally endowed pioneer, united with Diedre, who is wired for precision, creating a greater whole that afforded us to make an impact on churches, communities, cities, countries, and continents. We continue to grow and expand our capacity to help others grow and make a difference.

Throughout our years together we have constantly assessed our assets in connection to present and anticipated changes and challenges. It continues to be an amazing journey filled with miracles that both seed and stabilize our growing forward together. With courage, determination, and calculated efforts we strive for a life that honors God and fulfills our calling to serve.

We have often been challenged to appropriately appraise and value what we have and how it relates to our God destiny and present reality. Many times over we have availed ourselves of the opportunity to appreciate what God has given us to work with by affirming our trust in Him and His trust in us to get it done.

We have made amazing discoveries over the years through concrete experimentation as a learning model and method, meaning we jumped in and learned to fly-in the pursuit of shared dreams and destiny. We have also benefited greatly from more structured discovery of our natural and spiritual gifts, which we call our "God DNA," the synergy of what our Creator gives each of us at natural and spiritual birth. We are both certified human behavior consultants (CHBC), which equips us to help others discover their God DNA. It's time for you to make the discovery that connects you to the miracle in your house and to drive toward your destiny. Go to www.uniquelyyou.org/coach/Power2Become and discover your "God DNA."

It has been extremely valuable to finds ways within our means to experience time away with each other that refreshes us. It is these times when we are able to push past being overwhelmed by the enormity of the task, project, and/or call. Other times we must focus on acquiring the "right kind of help" to resource the vison, whether it be personal, ministry, or corporate organizations we have founded to achieve our God-given destiny.

Although we are very different in terms of personality, skill sets, fields of education, and experiences, we have successfully aligned based on our shared ability to produce plans, projects, and programs. We have created a work environment that affords us to be partners in life including marriage, ministry, and corporate pursuits. It is out of our developed capacity to work together by filling each other's gaps that we achieve an unconscious flow or synchrony. By being attached to our God mission growing together through the seasons of opportunity that flowed to us and the opportunities we've had to create, we are fulfilling what God has called us to individually and together.

We both intentionally use every occasion to teach and model a God-first lifestyle (Matthew 6:33) with mutual benefit exchange (Galatians 6:6). It is our hope that generations will learn how to overcome, adapt, and thrive in times of scarcity and abundance to achieve their God-given destinies.

We are continuously discovering that in order to sustain over the long haul, you must be sensitive and responsive to your own self-care and be honest about your true needs as a person: what makes you laugh, cry, and experience joy and so on.

We have found it tremendously valuable to become good stewards of whatever is entrusted to us throughout our lives and always to be in tune with *The earth is the*

Lord's, and the fulness thereof; the world, and they that dwell therein. For he hath founded it (Psalm 24:1–2). Therefore all our efforts are best lived out in context of His trust placed in us to become good stewards of all that is His. We are humbled by all that is entrusted to us.

We have engaged in business activity for much of our lives. Our entrepreneurial pursuits have been centered on providing training products that eliminate skill gaps, consulting services to enhance overall success, and speaking engagements to maximize and motivate peak performance.

We have delivered this mutual benefit exchange through conferences, books, one-on-one coaching, personal discovery workshops as certified human behavior consultants (www.Power2Become.org, www.Power2Become.com), and speaking engagements in both faith and business sectors as a certified John Maxwell team speaker, trainer, and coach (www.johncmaxwellgroup.com/josephwilson).

We also serve as healthy church coaches, helping local and national church organizations expand their reach. We have a team of certified church executives helping organizations to improve their systems. Joseph operates in a local and mobile format as a certified trainer with the Toler Leadership Institute and with The Power Institute at The Living Water Church International (www.livingwater2overflow.com), helping churches gain access to training and development that fosters growing forward.

It is our purpose to help as many individuals, teams, churches, and organizations as possible of all sectors and sizes to rise to the level of their greatness. We achieve this through partnered curriculum through Joseph's certifications with the John Maxwell Team as a speaker, trainer, coach, youth facilitator, and with the Toler Leadership Institute (www.Power2Become.org/leadership-development/). Diedre continues to grow forward with thirty-plus years of working with corporate executives, managers, and global teams in Fortune 100 companies and helping spin mergers navigate the future. She is also working toward her John Maxwell Team certification, to be completed in March 2020.

We are both licensed life insurance representatives in Ohio, helping individuals and families prepare for their long-term future and legacy. To set up a free financial needs analysis (FNA) and to establish peace of mind by ensuring your family's coverage, go to www.primerica.com/PBCT3.

We both have a long, rich history of working in mutual benefit exchange with companies to which we continue to contribute our time and talent. We do this for income as well as valuable experiences.

It is vitally important to apply yourself to your chosen field of endeavor. As my mentor, leadership expert John Maxwell teaches in *The Law of the Lid* that everything rises and falls on leadership. Whether you are the formal leader in your environment or the greatest influencer, you determine how far your organization can go.

"*Tell me, what do you have in your house?*" (2 Kings 4:2 NIV). Apply these *ten principles (or habits) of a breakthrough life,* which if embraced and applied to your life, can help you celebrate your value, advance your cause, and fulfill your purpose.

GET CONNECTED FOR IMPACT

- Speaking Inquiry Form—Ignite your personal and organizational growth
  http://Power2Become.org/newsite/events/events-2/my-bookings/

- Schedule Training—Are you and your organization prepared to sustain *growth*?
  http://Power2Become.org/leadership-development/

- Check Your Pulse—Are you healthy enough to *grow*?
  http://Power2Become.org/healthy-church-coaching/

- Discover Your Best Fit—The power of discovering and doing *you*
  https://uniquelyyou.org/coach/Power2Become

- Grow Healthy with Power 2 Become—Healthy people create healthy churches!
  https://totallifechanges.com/Power2Become

- Click Now to Become a Power Partner—Make a difference with your everyday life
  http://www.Power2Become.acndirect.com/

- Securing and Sustaining the Future—Set up a free financial needs analysis (FNA)
  http://www.primerica.com/PBCT3

Our Story

We enjoy a rich, working-together relationship. Nearly four decades of marriage and ministry have taken us to Germany, France, and all across the United States and Canada. We have developed a work synergy that positioned us to help grow and transition congregations as well as help startups gain footing and sustainability.

Much of what we have done stems from our shared desire to become missionaries, an interest developed as a newly married couple living in Germany, where I was assigned during my service in the military. We have managed to honor that heart and function in missionary-style ministry and service within each context of our various ministries. We have witnessed and directly influenced the salvation and transformation of individuals and families.

DESTINED TO UNITE

Our journey to each other and to ministry began more than four hundred years ago with our shared African ancestry in the regions of Cameroon/Congo, Benin/Togo, and Ghana. Our families were eventually part of the Great Migration from the southern U.S., with relatives from Alabama and Mississippi settling in Cleveland, Ohio. We came even closer as we attended rival junior high and senior high schools. Although we knew many of the same people, we don't recall encountering one another until I arrived on the campus of Baldwin-Wallace for fall football practice in 1981, having had to bounce back from a missed opportunity to attend a different university. Among the first students I met at college was Diedre, introduced to me by another student and mutual friend.

This student tapped me to replace him as the poster room manager charged with overseeing event advertisement; Diedre was a staff member. Thus, our working relationship began. Later, when I was set to conduct my first revival, Diedre helped me design flyers.

These years later, we would have never dreamed of the miraculous life that God has worked through us to create and deliver systems that reach and raise individuals, leaders, and organizations into kingdom ministry.

Though we are opposites as it relates to personality and style, we are both task oriented and wired to work on plans, programs, and events—but in very different ways. I am inclined to design, direct, and drive; Diedre is more likely to contemplate, analyze, and ensure accuracy and correctness of what needs to be done.

Academic challenges caused me to defer my college education and join the United States Army. Diedre was in her senior year and we married while I was home on leave. She deferred her degree to join me in Germany, where we lived for a time, building and discovering the miracles in our house. After living in Arizona for a time, we returned to Ohio and both completed our degree programs. Diedre graduated cum laude. I overcame past failure and graduated with awards for academic achievement at honors celebrations at two different colleges.

We eventually established two multicultural congregations and founded several for-profit and non-profit corporations that provide training, consulting, speaking, organizational development, and a myriad of other functions.

We have designed and developed training conferences and materials that have influenced thousands of lives and hundreds of churches. Living the principles in this book, we continue to innovate the future together and reinvent, reimagine, and reengineer ministry in answering God's call to make His business our business.

I have always been a dreamer, an innovator, one who creates and generates ideas and prototypes that need

Diedre's administrative and computer skills to make them both appealing and coherent.

GROWING FORWARD

In planting our first church, we had to take inventory of what we brought to the table that would help us reach and develop a group of people and organize them into a growing, functional church that works together. It was our belief that we had value to offer individuals and families that would transform their lives through Jesus Christ. It was then that we learned to effectively use our gifts, talents, and experiences and keep growing forward. We had to draw upon what we have learned by being in churches and what we have learned from our leaders to help us create a workable plan and develop an environment for a growing church.

We were young and full of faith with an understanding that God called us to establish a church on the west side of Cleveland. I became a bi-vocational pastor and continued to work full time to support our household and help support the infant ministry.

LIFE SHIFTS

However, God called me to full-time ministry, having two years earlier spoken to me that "the day will come when you will have to decide whether to keep going to your job or fulfill your ever-growing ministry schedule as pastor and become a national evangelist."

At this major life shift, I needed to go back to the beginning and rediscover "what's in my house" and now build a life and ministry without the security of a full-time job. This season required me to learn and to teach our church the biblical principles of mutual benefit exchange as taught by the apostle Paul in Galatians. 6:6: *Let him who is taught in the word share in all good things with him who teaches* (NKJV). This is what my pastor taught me before I left Germany in 1985.

My pastor also helped me overcome the miseducation and negative feelings about being compensated for ministry work. Some suggest that one should not be paid for working for the Lord as one would with other professions. He shared 1 Corinthians 9:5–11 and explained to me that fair exchange is not robbery. When you apply yourself to your craft as a profession and the resources are there, it is fair and appropriate to receive reasonable compensation to support yourself and your family.

He also counseled me that if you choose to, you can give it back after receiving what is right. However, the choice was mine. I was very young in age and ministry, but having received such teachings, I found they came back to me at the appropriate time to bless me and my family to think and behave in biblical and healthy ways concerning ministry compensation.

GENEROSITY BEGETS GENEROSITY

We currently serve in ways of developed capacity to initiate, recover, and creatively turn things around in any setting, helping leaders and organizations grow forward.

It has been our intentional effort to engage ministry as stewards of our Father's business, modeling mutual benefit exchange for generations to come (Galatians 6:6; 1 Corinthians 9; Romans 15:27). We have embodied "*help* that *grows* with *you*," the motto of Power 2 Become Ministries (Power2Become.org), a 501(c)3 organization that focuses on leadership training, church development, and personal discovery. Power 2 Become Ministries has grown from concept to a viable and respected organization.

We've experienced other changes in which God once again called me away from the security of pastoral compensation into evangelistic ministry. This kind of ministry is often regulated by activity and opportunity, which can be sporadic and very scary.

It was during this season that I had to reinvent myself by growing in capacity, diversity of gifts, and intentionally expand my ministry platform, which had a direct impact on my income.

We regularly level up our skills, abilities, education, and training to match our God-given mission within the corporations that we have created. This allows us to have proper exchange of goods and services to sustain our lives while doing our Father's business.

We continue to live a God-first life based on Matthew 6:33 and experience God's fulfillment of His promise to sustain us. Having learned the habits of good stewardship together, we can keep our focus on our purpose.

I must admit that it can be scary in growing to the point of trusting God and trusting that people know, follow, and obey the Scriptures in relation to mutual benefit exchange with those who serve in ministry. I've discovered it's more about learning to *behave in our belief in biblical principles* rather than focusing on what we get.

Give away your life; you'll find life given back, but not merely given back—given back with bonus and blessing. Giving, not getting, is the way. Generosity begets generosity (Luke 6:38 MSG).

We pray that this book will bless your life as it has ours and help you also to *Discover the Miracle in Your House.*

About the Authors

Photo Credit: Rebecca Lynn Photography, LLC

Joseph Wilson is pastor/founder of The Living Water Church International; CEO and founder of Power 2 Become Ministries, Inc., and bishop/apostolic leader of The Power Network International. He is a certified speaker, trainer, coach, and youth facilitator with the John Maxwell Team and trainer with the Toler Leadership Institute. He is the author of *Walking Toward Christ with the Apostle Paul: A Journey from Faith to Faith* and *Preaching Pews: An Everyday Believer's Guide to Faith Sharing,* and coauthor of

Discover the Miracle in Your House: 10 Principles of a Break-through Life.

Diedre Wilson is vice president of administrative affairs, a certified healthy church coach, and a certified human behavior consultant (CHBC) with Power 2 Become Ministries, Inc., founding board member of The Living Water Church International and The Power Network International, editor-in-chief of Powerful Moments Internet Radio Broadcast on WCANRadio.com, editor of *Walking Toward Christ with the Apostle Paul: A Journey from Faith to Faith* and *Preaching Pews: An Everyday Believer's Guide to Faith Sharing,* and coauthor of *Discover the Miracle in Your House: 10 Principles of a Breakthrough Life.*

Made in the USA
Lexington, KY
13 November 2019

56954261R00061